Six Minute
Homeschool Day

Shorten Your Day
Sweeten Your Time

Tamara L. Chilver

TLC Editions
Fort Myers, Florida

Simplify Your Homeschool Day
Shorten Your Day
Sweeten Your Time

Information on Tamara L. Chilver's resources
can be found on-line at **www.teachingwithtlc.com**.

ISBN: 978-1490928265
Published by TLC Editions
Fort Myers, FL

A special thanks to:
Leslie Simpson- cover design
Haleigh Katwaroo- editing

Table of Contents

Introduction

Who could use a little extra time as a parent and home educator? I can see your hands shooting up as I write this. As a mom of five, I can testify that even a few extra minutes a day can seem like a treasure in this busy season of life.

I am very passionate about encouraging fellow home educators. It is something I tend to pour my heart into and I love every minute of it. Balancing this while chasing around two active toddlers who are into everything and homeschooling three older children, I have still found time to pursue my additional interests. I often get asked how in the world do I have time to do it all. After teaching 20 years and lots of God's amazing grace, I have learned several time-saving tricks that have freed me to have the extra time to pursue my passions.

God's Word tells us in Psalm 90:12, "Teach us to number our days aright, that we may gain a heart of wisdom."

This scripture teaches us that every minute in every day matters, and God can give us wisdom in everything we do. Being effective teachers can help our children learn more during school time, as well as give them more time to explore, discover, and enjoy the learning process.

Chapter 1
Practical Tips to Shorten Your School Day

I am thrilled to be able to share with you over 100 simple teaching tips in this book I have learned during my homeschool journey that have shortened my children's school day. Some of these tips you may have heard before but you may benefit from a gentle reminder while most of my other tips may actually surprise you. Grab your favorite highlighter and let's get started!

Get organized.

This may sound pretty basic, but the success of your homeschool experience depends on being prepared and organized. Having a sense of things being in order will help you adjust to the many unforeseen things that can pop up and throw you off course.

Declutter your stash of homeschool resources even if this means taking off a day or two of homeschooling to get organized. Remember, teachers get planning days during the school year to get caught up and organized.

Never underestimate the power of post-its. Use these sticky notes on work for corrections, reminders, and rewards. Use horizontal file stackers, file folders, plastic bins, and shelves. Avoid wasting time hunting for paper, pens, and other school supplies by having them all accessible in one location.

When school time is over, put everything away and include some time to get organized for the next day. There is no way to predict what tomorrow will bring so be prepared. Additionally, an overall sense of organization allows you to adjust for impromptu outings and teachable moments that are some of the benefits of homeschooling.

Establish a routine.

Establishing a routine goes along with organization. Children function best when they have a routine. There are varying degrees to this but at least have a basic routine, such as a consistent time to begin school each day. Keep your routine from being so structured that it is mechanical and doesn't allow you to enjoy the many freedoms that come along with homeschooling. But don't let it be so loosely structured that chaos reigns. Find what works for your family and then stick with it.

Use only the best.

Just as a carpenter uses only the best tools available, you should use only the best learning tools. Do your research. There are plenty of websites that review materials and curriculum. My friend Heidi at www.homeschool-how-to.com is a veteran homeschool mom who has reviewed many different products if you need a great place to get started.

Get involved in a homeschool group and learn from others what resources they've used. Some of the best ideas I have used in homeschooling I have learned about from fellow home educators.

Strive for quality, not quantity. Sort through everything you have accumulated and discard anything that is "just okay." Your child deserves only the best, and your time teaching is invaluable. For example, if a book has "one good chapter," give it away. It just takes up space, clutters up your life, and is another thing you have to remember to use.

View purchasing wonderful learning tools as an investment. You only get one short childhood to teach. Look for excellent resources that reveal the thrilling part of learning new things. For instance, if you use science books, make sure they contain vivid photography and truly interesting text.

Get back to the basics.

As home educators we can often create extra stress for ourselves as we begin to plan our school year. We do this out of love for our children by wanting to provide the highest quality education for them and part of this is finding the best resources and teaching tools.

This advice sounds simple but have you ever attended a large homeschool convention? It is quite overwhelming. The homeschooling market is a billion dollar industry, and we are the target audience in that market. A curriculum will sound perfect for our child as we browse a vendor's booth and listen to the sales pitch until we walk to the next booth or talk to a parent who has used something else. We easily become confused and frustrated. With all these teaching materials at our reach, it is very easy to attempt to squeeze in everything.

This is why it is imperative to concentrate on the core subjects- reading, writing, & math. Simply put, your school day should be centered on these basic subject areas. When the school day becomes off balanced with too many other subjects and electives, you need to reprioritize and reschedule your day. Take time to regroup and gain a clear focus again by getting back to the basics.

Make reading a top priority.

Reading is the most important subject because it overlaps into all subject areas. A strong foundation in reading will lead to success in other subjects. This is why you should spend most of your instructional time in the primary grades preparing your child to become a strong, independent reader. The faster your child can read while still comprehending, the quicker he will be able to read and complete assignments in other subject areas, too.

When your child can read well independently, continue reading aloud to him since reading aloud is the best thing parents can do to help their children become avid and strong readers. Reading aloud also helps children improve their vocabulary, spelling, grammar, attention span, comprehension, and listening skills. The Commission on Reading states, "The single most important activity for building the knowledge required for success in school is reading aloud to children." This research should make you want to grab a book and cuddle with your child right now. Remember you are investing your time in his future.

Combine lessons and subjects.

Kill two birds with one stone by combining separate lessons. For example, there is no need to practice handwriting as a separate subject after your child has learned how to write letters correctly. You can evaluate his handwriting in his writing assignments. Also, your child can type some writing assignments to practice typing skills instead of teaching typing separately.

Overlap subjects, such as giving writing assignments that correlate with your child's science, literature, and social studies lessons. This method increases your child's knowledge of the subject matter and retention of the content while developing critical thinking skills.

Expand subjects.

Some subjects can be stretched out. A short-cut method is to divide a book in half, and use the same book for two years. This not only saves you time but money, too!

For example, English/grammar curriculum can be very repetitive. Complete one to two lessons per week. The goal is to have your child apply the rules he learns, so get him writing the other two days a week. When writing, children are learning English and grammar rules and will retain them better than when isolating the same skills in worksheets and textbooks, which brings me to my next time-saving tip.

Eliminate busy work.

Research has repeatedly shown for over a century that busy work does not increase retention. In the *Read-Aloud Handbook*, Jim Release reveals that there is no correlation between the number of worksheets a child completes in school and his academic success. I still use worksheets and workbooks occasionally to review or reinforce concepts, but I do not use them as my main teaching tool.

Flip-flop subjects.

Alternate some subjects every other semester or school year, such as teaching social studies one semester or year and science the next. This same method can be applied to electives, such as foreign language, music, and art classes.

This frees up time to dive more into these subjects instead of rushing through to cover every subject area each school day. This approach involves a smaller amount of preparation for the parent and is less confusing for the child.

Give your child choices.

You can let your child choose which picture book to read next or which order to complete his school work. I sometimes narrow down the curriculum choices for the year and will let my oldest son have the final choice. When you give your child some choices, he will take more ownership of his school work and naturally develop a passion for learning.

Test first.

One quick way to assess if your child already knows the content is to have your child complete the chapter test. This may sound backwards but it will save a lot of time. For instance, give an oral pretest for spelling and only practice and assign work for the words your child does not know how to spell. Why spend time practicing words your child already knows how to spell?

Use quizzes and end-of-chapter tests in math, science, and social studies to determine what your child already knows. Just cover the material he needs to learn and move on to another challenge. There's really no need to stretch out the school day to cover material your child has already mastered.

Avoid too much repetition.

There is much truth to "less is more." Your child is more likely to complete his work correctly when he is not overwhelmed by a large number of problems.

Textbooks always give you more than you need, and there is no reason to complete every problem on every page. This is especially true in math. Educators usually shorten the number of math problems or assign the even/odd problems. If your child needs more practice, he can complete the other problems at a later time.

Use a timer.

This time-saving tip will only work for certain children-the competitive type that enjoy playing games. Set a timer and challenge your child to finish his assignment before the timer goes off. You have to negotiate ahead of time on a reward. I sometimes add ten minutes to bedtime or reward with a dollar or a treat. I especially like using the timer when my children are practicing math drills. My kids love games and challenges so this trick works like a charm for them. However, some children may get stressed from using a timer, and it can actually lengthen the time it takes them to complete the assignment.

I also use a timer for a ten minute clean-up after school is over. Everyone, including my little ones, picks up the house for ten minutes. When the timer goes off, I inspect each section that was preassigned to a child. If that area is clean, the child can have free time.

Relax.

If you sense your child getting frustrated with a particular skill, do not panic but take a break. It is important to realize that most learning occurs in waves. These peaks of learning are referred to as "light bulb moments." It is when your child grasps a concept that you have worked on for days, weeks, months, or even years.

Some children need a lot of variety and repetition, while others seem to almost teach themselves. Take your time and progress at your child's own pace. Most importantly, do not rush to keep your child on "grade level." Children can catch up on years of learning in a matter of months.

There is not any conclusive evidence early readers will excel faster and perform better in future school years when compared to late readers. A recent study has proven that teaching children to read from age five is not likely to make that child any more successful at reading than a child who learns reading later, from age seven. Dr. Sebastian Suggate states the pressure for children to learn to read at the age of 5 is unnecessary. Late readers catch up with their peers by the age of 11.

For example, I once taught a child in third grade who was reading on a first grade level. He had a "learning spurt" which moved him to the head of the class for reading by the end of the school year. This is a great reminder not to stretch out your school day to push your child forward. As home educators, we need to trust that our children will succeed if we provide the right learning atmosphere and tools.

Take a step backwards.

Sometimes there may not be a developmental issue but an underlying problem. When your child is consistently struggling with a concept, take a step backwards and analyze the problem.

One example of focusing on what is causing the hindrance in your child's learning is if he is struggling with fractions, go back and review the multiplication and division facts. These facts set the foundation for fractions. One step backwards may lead to two steps forward.

Avoid over-scheduling.

Too many times in my homeschool journey I have created extra stress for myself by over-scheduling. Imagine if you filled an 8 ounce glass to the rim with 8 ounces of your favorite drink. Next, you had to walk to another room to sit and enjoy your drink. While walking, you become worried and maybe even anxious about spilling your drink because you allowed yourself no gap to account for movement.

We commonly do this in planning our homeschool day. In our lesson plans, the school day looks perfectly coordinated to the minute but then real life happens. There may be a knock at the door, a sick child to care for, an unexpected phone call, or even a teething toddler. The results are anger, frustration, and sometimes tears. This is why you should intentionally plan a gap of time (your wiggle room) each day to allow for the distractions that will occur.

Use bookmarks.

I have evaluated hundreds of portfolios over the years for homeschool, and the most common tip I tell fellow moms is to use a bookmark. You are not in a race to the end of the school year. You don't need to work double time to finish the book or curriculum. Remember, you are teaching your child, not the curriculum. Use a bookmark at the end of the year, and begin where you left off the following school year.

Many parents feel a compulsive need to complete every assignment on every page in every book. I'll let you in on an insider's secret; classroom teachers never finish the entire book. Publishing companies always provide more than what is needed. If you want to complete the curriculum, but the school year has ended, insert a bookmark and pick up where you left off when school resumes.

I believe most home educators struggle with this, and I must admit I was one of them. There was even a school year when my oldest son only made it through half of a math book because he was struggling with certain concepts. I used my bookmark, and we continued using the same book the following school year.

Do not rush your child to get through the book. Teach for mastery. Homeschooling is about comprehension, not completion.

Learn to pick and choose.

It is not the quantity of time but the quality of education that counts. Thirty minutes of active learning is equivalent to several hours of passive learning. It is okay to skip pages or even chapters in your curriculum. Maybe you would rather spend extra time on teaching something else, or your child has already mastered those concepts.

If you are striving to teach everything, a packed curriculum can be a mile wide but only an inch deep. By concentrating on what is relevant and interesting to your child, you allow more time to dive into meaningful topics and your child will want to become immersed with knowledge.

Get your child moving to improve learning.

Thanks to advances in research on how the brain works, we now know that most of the brain is activated during physical activity. From some of this research, I learned that too much sitting is detrimental to learning. Eric Jensen, author of a number of books on brain-based learning, and Rae Pica, author of *More Movement, Smarter Kids* say it best, "Sitting for more than 10 minutes at a stretch reduces our awareness of physical and emotional sensations and increases fatigue resulting in reduced concentration. Movement, on the other hand, increases blood vessels that allow for the delivery of oxygen, water, and glucose to the brain. This can't help but optimize the brain's performance."

As a mother of four active boys, I have become a master of incorporating movement into our learning activities. Whenever your child needs a break from sitting when completing assignments, try the "Get Moving Approach" and implement one of the following activities.

•Snap and clap letters to spelling words.

•Jump on a mini-trampoline while practicing math facts and spelling words.

•Ride a stationary bike, rock in a rocking chair, or swing in a porch swing while reading aloud.

•Roll a ball back and forth to each other, or have your child bounce a ball as he spells words or practices math facts.

•Assign a simple task to keep your child focused when you read aloud. Have him raise his hand or touch his nose when he hears a certain word.

•Stand up to complete work. He can even take turns standing on one leg.

Recognize your child may need background noise to study.

I often wondered how my husband could study in college with the radio on and still graduate as valedictorian of his graduating class. If I even heard the hum of a ceiling fan, I would lose all concentration while studying. I even remember placing my hands over my ears to block out every bit of background noise.

Thankfully, I remembered how my husband and I studied differently in college when my oldest son began to study like his father. While my son was in middle school, I would walk into his room when he was completing his schoolwork. He would have the television on low in the background or he would have on headphones playing music. He said he needed background noise to focus.

I had to remind myself that his father did very well in school with the same study habits. If I had not seen beforehand how background noise can improve learning in some people, I would have required him to turn it off. This would have made it more difficult for my son to study and added more time to his school day. Even though I cannot explain or understand it, I have to trust that God wired us all differently and let it be.

Disguise learning.

No matter how much fun you try to make it, most children will have one or more subjects they dislike. Your teaching time during these subjects may feel like it drags on and on. So, what do you do now? Your job is to disguise it.

If your child does not like to eat vegetables, you may try to disguise them by adding cheese to their broccoli, ranch dressing for dipping carrot sticks, or peanut butter to celery sticks. You can even make a vegetable casserole. The point is you still have your child eat vegetables, you just disguise them.

We can apply the same principal to learning by using a creative approach. For example, if your child is tired of practicing his spelling words by writing them out or spelling them aloud, here are some fun ways to practice spelling that lead to true learning.

•Use toothpicks, pretzel sticks, or straws to form the letters in the words.

•Use items, such as beans and Cheerios, to form the letters in the words.

•Use flashlights to spell the words on a wall in a dark room.

•Use alphabet magnets to make the words on the refrigerator.

•Paint the words with watercolors or finger paints.

Have your child act, dance, or do jumping jacks for the letters in the words. This is my favorite spelling activity to do with my boys when they can't sit another minute. They love it because they are moving, and I love it because they are learning!

For more creative spelling ideas, check out my book *101 Ways to Make Spelling Fun.* The ultimate goal of disguising learning is to think out of the box, but don't lose track of the box because you may need it for a school project.

Delegate

Homeschooling is a team effort, and everyone should pitch in. Don't try to do it all. For instance, my children complete several chores daily. My older children read to my younger ones while I am grading assignments. My husband helps teach our children science. Go Chilver team!

Break it down.

When you are teaching your child a difficult concept or a large unit study, try breaking up his assignments into smaller, "bite-size" portions. If your child is learning math facts, only teach one set a day or even a week. If your child still has a hard time grasping the facts, teach only a couple of facts per day. This allows your child to conquer the small bits of information first and then put them altogether later.

You can also incorporate mini-breaks while teaching difficult concepts. For instance, have him complete a math assignment and then go for a bike ride around the block. Have your child read a chapter in his required reading assignment and then eat a snack. By giving your child breaks, you will increase his ability to focus and complete his work faster.

Take advantage of gaps.

You may not realize that there are blocks of time in your daily routine that you can use for homeschool activities. One way I utilize gaps is I have my younger children complete their handwriting assignments while I make breakfast. This way I can oversee their work and I am available if they need assistance, but there is no need for me to sit next to them during that time.

My children also watch an educational television program or video while eating lunch. Filling these blocks of time with learning activities really adds up. For instance, watching a science program that my kids love, such as *The Magic School Bus* or *Wild Kratts*, while eating lunch equals two and a half hours of extra science per week.

Use checklists.

This method will eliminate your child waiting on you in between assignments, which equals less time to complete his school work. Checklists give your child purpose and direction, and they enable him to see an end to the homeschool day. This motivates your child to work harder and stay on task at a steady pace.

You can use a very basic checklist for younger children with 4-5 subject areas. Have your child place a sticker next to each task when he completes it.

Older children can check off their assignments as they complete them. Here is a checklist that my middle boys used this school year.

___ Chores

___ Calendar/Prayers

___ Bible

___ Reading

___ Grammar

___ Handwriting

___ Math

___ Writing

___ Piano

___ History Unit Study

My kids have to complete their checklists to have any free time activities, such as playing outside with their friends or building Lego creations. Since they can visually see themselves getting closer to their reward (free time), my boys will work extra hard to finish.

Checklists provide a way for your child to be accountable for his work, and he will gain a feeling of accomplishment at the end of the day. In addition, the completed checklists can be easily placed in a binder for your school records.

Provide free time choices.

If you are using the checklist method or any other incentive that uses free time as a motivational tool, have a variety of choices established. Many children will fill their free time with video games, television, surfing the Internet, and so on. The main reason we strive to finish our schoolwork in a timely manner is so everyone can have extra time to pursue their own interests (moms included).

A simple technique to help monitor your child's free time is to brainstorm a list together of all of the things your child has your permission to do after school is over. This list can be a fun "Top Ten" list that is posted where your child can easily refer to it. This will also help your child refrain from saying the dreaded words, "I'm bored."

Some examples that may make your child's Top Ten list could be: working on a home-based business, reading, playing outside, emailing a pen pal, calling a relative, serving others, playing an instrument, making creations from materials (such as Legos or Tinker toys), playing board games, creating art projects, cooking a special meal, gardening, and fishing.

Add an incentive.

People of all ages like to be rewarded for hard work. Think about when you have received a reward for extra hard work as an adult, such as a pay check, bonus, vacation, special recognition, or even a heartfelt letter of thanks. You were more than likely thrilled.

If your child has become resistant in completing his work in a timely manner, simply use incentives to encourage him. I have used incentives in the classroom as well as in my own home teaching my children. The truth is they really work!

One incentive I have used at home with my younger children is taping a $5.00 bill to the back of their workbooks. You should have seen how fast my boys worked through their phonics curriculum. My husband even caught them in bed with flashlights at night trying to finish them as fast as they could! They literally finished the entire year of phonics workbooks in just two months.

I have adapted this technique and taped a printed photo of an item they really wanted, such as a Lego set, to the back of their math workbooks. Since the reward was for an entire year of work, it was larger. Again, my boys finished their math curriculum in a short amount of time. They spent the rest of the school year practicing problem-solving and learning how to relate math to real-life situations. It was wonderful!

Choose an incentive that will motivate your child, and watch your child be excited to complete his work.

Utilize peak learning times.

Your child has a time during the day when he can complete work faster than usual. Even though these times can vary, most kids focus best right after breakfast. If your child is struggling to complete a subject, use his peak learning time to help him out. For instance, if your child is slow in completing math and he is typically more focused in the morning, assign math first.

It may take a week or two of experimenting to find your child's peak learning time. Assign a subject area that usually takes your child longer to complete at a different time each day. Watch closely to see how your child is able to focus.

One of my boys has a hard time concentrating during the day but is very focused at night. Now that doesn't mean I am going to homeschool every night on top of every day with my other children, but I have learned to take advantage of his peak learning times with checklists. My son completes as many assignments as he can independently do each evening. He sleeps in a little later than my other children and then we work together on the assignments that are left after breakfast. Most of our school days go very smoothly with this approach but could easily turn into a disaster if I forced him to complete all of his assignments in the morning and early afternoon.

My son happens to be a night owl like his mom so I am extra receptive to making adjustments to accommodate his peak learning times.

Summer Learning Adventures

The average child loses two months of learning each summer, which is commonly referred to as the "summer slide." To prevent spending weeks reviewing in the beginning of each school year, continue to do educational activities (with a fun twist) in the summer months.

The summer months are great for spending time on recreational reading, field trips, art projects, science labs, computer games, electives, subjects that make you feel rushed during the school year, and skills that may need more practice, such as problem-solving. It is also nice when you want to take off extra time in the school year- no guilt!

Steer clear of the "Terrible Too's."

Cramming *too* much work in the school day and teaching concepts *too* soon often leads to burn out for parent and child. It is a parent's natural inclination to want your child to succeed and sometimes we can push too hard. Follow your child's natural learning process and avoid teaching *too* much *too* soon.

No more X's.

When your child answers something incorrectly, circle the problem/question and have him redo it. When you use an "X," you are telling your child that he has missed it and to move on. As home educators, we want our children to go back and correctly answer the problem to master the concept being taught.

Avoid using the color red to grade with.

Even though red was the color of choice by most educators while I was growing up, it is actually a threatening color for children since red is typically associated with aggression and stress. In fact, most schools no longer allow teachers to use red for grading.

My personal favorite colors to use while grading are hot pink, lime green, bright purple, and turquoise blue. You can also choose your child's favorite color to use.

How do these grading tips save time? When you use "X" and red ink, you are subconsciously encouraging your child to stop. For instance, what do you do when you see a large X or a red stoplight? We want our children to move forward. Simple changes like color choices and circling incorrect answers encourages your child to go back and try again without any hesitation.

Use color to your advantage.

Have you ever wondered why your little girl can't sit still at the table in your red kitchen, or why your son can't stay focused on an assignment while completing it at a desk in his orange room? Since we are discussing color, I want to share some really cool tips I learned while attending a homeschool workshop. These tips opened my eyes to how powerful color can be in teaching.

Colors send signals to the brain without us even thinking about it. Some help us focus and some are extremely distracting. As a parent, it's important to know how color influences learning and what colors are best for specific learning environments. Let's explore colors and learn how to use them for your advantage, especially during your homeschool time.

While pale yellow and pink provide a calm and happy learning environment, the hot dog colors (bright yellow, orange, and red) need to be avoided as much as possible in your child's homeschool area.

Bright yellow excites the brain and body. It makes people want to move and talk. Although it is a color that represents happiness (ex. smiley face), it is not a good choice for a room where a child needs to complete schoolwork. You won't be very happy as a parent when your child is talking instead of writing or reading.

The color orange represents energy and is probably the worst color to paint a place that you want your child to sit still and complete his homework. You might find him dancing instead.

Shades of red can actually increase your heart rate, and too much red can be downright distracting. If you send your child to complete school work in a room that has red accents (such as a pillow or curtain), don't be surprised if your child takes awhile to complete his assignment and then comes out asking for a snack.

Red often triggers hunger. Think about the colors that are used for fast food restaurant signs. You may not have been hungry until you looked at the sign. Suddenly, you have the urge to park and grab a meal.

This is not a coincidence. Combined with orange and yellow, these colors make you want to eat and leave quickly (and be happy while doing so).

However, these hot dog colors can be used as positive teaching tools. Research shows that an occasional bold stroke of yellow, orange, or red attracts the learner's attention to details. No wonder most highlighters are bright yellow. These colors can be useful for alerting your child to specific points of knowledge or new concepts.

Use mnemonics.

Mnemonics is the art of assisting the memory by using a system of artificial aids like rhymes, rules, phrases, diagrams, acronyms, and other devices. These are fantastic for recalling names, dates, facts, and figures. You can even invent your own mnemonics for memorization.

Here are some of my favorite mnemonics I have used when teaching in a classroom, tutoring, and home-schooling.

Three Main Insect Parts

HAT

Head
Abdomen
Thorax

Order of Planets

My (Mercury)
Very (Venus)
Educated (Earth)
Mother (Mars)
Just (Jupiter)
Served (Saturn)
Us (Uranus)
Nine (Neptune)
Pizzas (Pluto)

*Pluto is no longer recognized as a planet so you can substitute the Nine for Nachos.

Vertebrates

FARM B

Fish
Amphibians
Reptiles
Mammals
Birds

For Order of Operations in Math

Please (Parentheses)
Excuse (Exponents)
My (Multiplication)
Dear (Division)
Aunt (Addition)
Sally (Subtraction)

Division Procedures

Daddy (Divide)
Mother (Multiply)
Sister (Subtract)
Brother (Bring Down)

Mode & Median

The **mode** is the value there are the **most** of. "Mode" and "Most" have the same starting 2 letters.

The **median** splits the data down the middle, like the **median strip in a road**.

Great Lakes

HOMES

Huron
Ontario
Michigan
Erie
Superior

Parts of an Atom

PEN

Protons
Electrons
Neutrons

Conjunctions

BOY SAT (with) BEN

But
Or
Yet
So
And
Then
Both...and
Either...or
Neither...nor

Liquid Measurements

The length of each word reveals the measure's size.
(shortest word- smallest size)

cup
pint
quart
gallon

Lines of the Treble Staff (from bottom to top)

EGBDF

Every Good Boy Does Fine

Spaces of the Treble Staff (from bottom to top)

FACE

Spaces in the Bass Clef

All
Cows
Eat
Grass

Colors of the Rainbow

ROY G. BIV

Red
Orange
Yellow
Green
Blue
Indigo
Violet

Metric Units of Measure in Order

King Henry Doesn't Usually Drink Cold Milk.

Kilo
Hecto
Deca
Units [meter, liter, gram]
Deci
Centi
Milli

Roman Numerals

I =1, V = 5, and X = 10

I View X-rays.

L = 50, C = 100, D = 500 and M = 1000

Lucy Can't Drink Milk.

I have created colorful printable posters for each of these mnemonics. I print them on cardstock and use them as visual teaching aides during the school year. You can find them on my site.

Check out *Every Good Boy Deserves Fudge* by Roy Evans for a quick-reference resource filled with mnemonics for specific subjects.

Maximize brain power with water.

The brain is approximately eighty percent water. Although a number of beverages seem to satisfy your child's thirst, water is the only beverage that will also quench his brain. Drinks that contain caffeine are diuretics and actually reduce water in the body. Being thirsty causes learning problems because thirst increases cortisol levels. This makes paying attention to tasks more difficult. Within five minutes of drinking plain water, cortisol levels decrease and attention levels increase.

Your child is naturally dehydrated when he wakes up in the morning. This is why it is imperative to have your child drink one glass of water, in addition to his breakfast drink, every morning before homeschooling. Remind your child to drink water throughout the school day, especially when he may be having a hard time focusing.

This is one of those teaching tips I wish I had learned twenty years ago when I was teaching in the classroom. The effects of water are so visible with my own children, especially my middle child. When he becomes distracted while completing his school work and can no longer concentrate, I ask him to drink a big glass of water and I can see the difference in his ability to focus within minutes. It makes a huge difference!

Boost your child's brain power with protein.

Learning requires optimum health and brain function. If a child is eating the wrong foods or foods that are deficient in the proper nutrients, his ability to learn will be compromised. Parents can enhance a child's learning ability by providing nutritious snacks and meals. Children who eat healthy meals are more likely to have better concentration, problem solving skills, and hand-eye coordination. They are also more alert and creative.

The high concentration of processed sugar in a typical breakfast makes your child's brain groggy and will make paying attention much more difficult. Your child will avoid the "learning grogginess" by cutting back on high-sugar carbohydrates and increasing proteins. Here are examples of sources of protein to include with your child's snack or meal: peanut butter on toast, melted cheese on bread, hardboiled eggs, meats, yogurt, and cottage cheese mixed with fruit. The key is to balance the proteins and carbohydrates.

Go outside.

There is a clear link between being outside and increased learning. Fresh air and moderate sunlight can boost brain power. It stimulates more production of red blood cells, which increases the amount of oxygen in your blood. It also increases the production of endorphins and serotonin in your brain as well as Vitamin D in your skin, which makes you feel refreshed and focused. Being in small amounts of sunlight can also help you sleep better since it will increase your melatonin output at night. Melatonin is a natural hormone made by our bodies which enhances sleep. So the next time you have nice weather, take your books outside.

On a side note, research has shown that boys often have a difficult time concentrating if they are too warm. Girls are the opposite and have a hard time focusing when they are too cold. Keep that in mind when you venture outdoors to study.

Make sleep a priority.

Did you know that most new material learned during the day is moved to long-term memory during sleep? This fascinating fact shows how sleep is closely connected to learning.

Staying up too late is a common pitfall for children. Did you know the National Sleep Foundation recommends elementary-age children sleep a minimum of ten to eleven hours per night? Stop to calculate if your child is getting enough sleep.

Tired children are often cranky and fussy, and they become easily frustrated. Sleep enables the brain to encode new information and store it properly. The parts of the brain that control emotions, decision-making, and social interactions slow down dramatically during sleep, which allows optimal performance when awake.

Children thrive on a regular sleep schedule, even on weekends. Your child should go to sleep and wake up at roughly the same time every day. Fight the urge to let him stay up late and sleep in on weekends. What you are doing is asking your child to live in two different time zones- a weekday zone and a weekend zone. As a result, your child gets perpetual jet lag.

What your child eats and drinks affects how he sleeps. One of the keys to a restful night's sleep is to get your child's brain calmed. Limit your child's intake of caffeine at least six hours before bedtime. If your child prefers a snack before going to sleep, give him foods that induce the body's production of serotonin, the neurotransmitter that slows down nerve traffic so your child's brain is not so busy. Some of the following bedtime snacks induce sleep: cottage cheese, milk, turkey, cheese, peanuts, hard-boiled eggs, whole-grain cereal, and oatmeal. Snacks should be eaten no later than one hour before bedtime.

Tap into God's power.

I am going to end this chapter with the best time-saving tip of all. I cannot imagine trying to vacuum my house without plugging the vacuum into the wall. It may still work unplugged while I push it since it has the beater bar circulating and picking up large clumps of debris. But it is MUCH more effective when I plug it into its power source. The same is true for homeschooling. So much more could be accomplished in a smaller amount of time if I use the main power source.

This sounds so basic to me, but I still need to be reminded on a regular basis to plug into God's power. I get distracted, overwhelmed, side-tracked, and even derailed sometimes and forget to apply this simple, yet very powerful tip.

There have been several occasions where I have hit a wall in homeschooling. I become a little anxious and start calling other homeschool moms, reading blog articles from veteran home educators, or even researching options myself all in my quest for the answer. In the midst of this, I often forget to first seek Him who has all the answers. You think I would be a natural at this after homeschooling for 15 years, but I am definitely an example of a work in progress.

God knows our children better than we do, and He has a plan for our children. Jeremiah 29:11 states, "For I know the plans I have for you," declares the Lord.

Be sure to plug into God's power daily to maximize your teaching time for your child.

Chapter 2
Communication Skills that Nurture Learning

Have you ever tried to unlock a door and the key will not work? After several failed attempts, you discover you were using the wrong key all along. Sometimes, you may need to grab another key when it comes to opening the doors of communication with your child.

Motivation is the primary key to learning. Your child needs your love, encouragement, approval, and affirmation. In this chapter, you will learn several techniques that will help you communicate clearly with your child and unlock his enthusiasm for learning.

Do not compare.

Consistently emphasize that everyone has strengths and weaknesses. God did not create us to be good at everything but to efficiently use the unique gifts that He has given us. Make sure your child knows he is measured against his own abilities, not against a sibling's or a friend's abilities.

Use constructive criticism.

Correct the behavior of your child in a non-authoritarian way. Constructive criticism is tactful, and its purpose is not to hurt feelings but to help your child understand a lesson that he can grow from. Always point out the "why" of what your child did wrong or could do better, and give an explanation as to why it's wrong. Show mercy and do not embarrass your child. This includes criticizing your child's learning in front of siblings and friends. Finally, ask your child what he thinks he will do differently next time.

Compliment before you criticize.

You can do this by stating something positive before the negative. For example, "I like the way you wrote this paragraph with complete sentences and a consistent theme, but I feel it would be easier for the reader to relate to the character if you were to add more details."

Many educators like to use the "sandwich approach." With this approach, you praise, correct, and then praise. It is wonderful for children who are extra sensitive and tend to be perfectionists. It is a subtle method and most children do not even realize they are being corrected when you use this technique.

Repeat directions.

I might have to repeat this simple tip over and over for you to believe how effective this tip is. ☺ Think about a time your child spent time completing an assignment but did it incorrectly because of not understanding the instructions. Do you recall his frustration when he had to repeat the entire assignment again?

Have your child repeat the directions back to you when giving steps or directions for assignments. This helpful hint will enable your child to work more independently and avoid unnecessary mistakes.

Ask open-ended questions.

Closed-ended questions require a yes or no answer. Open-ended questions invite your child to express himself in his own words. By asking questions this way, the parent is able to gather information while the child develops a greater understanding of the material. Some examples of open-ended questions include:

•What does that mean to you?

•What do you think will happen next in the story?

•What is the next step in solving this problem?

•How did you make that choice?

•Would you tell me more about your answer?

•What would you do differently next time?

Pay close attention.

In a national survey, more than half the children who participated said that when they talked, their parents often didn't give them a chance to explain themselves. Parents, effective communication begins with listening well. Carve out time to give your child your undivided attention.

One important way to show your child you are listening is to make eye contact. This means not looking at the television, your phone, or computer. I often remind my children to look at me when I am talking, so I know they are paying close attention to what I am saying.

Another key part of listening is not interrupting your child and finishing his sentences. Give your child some extra time to express his concerns or answers, even if you think you know what he's going to say. This is my biggest communication weakness because when I speak, I typically get to the point fairly fast. On the other hand, one of my sons tends to ramble and sometimes it takes him awhile to get to the point. Without realizing it, I would often complete his sentences until I saw his frustration one day. Now I work really hard on listening patiently and attentively and not interrupting him.

Celebrate the positive.

There are always victories in learning that we can celebrate and use to encourage our children to greater success. Some of them may be small, such as mastering several sight words. Other achievements, such as completing a book report independently, are larger. But all deserve celebration. If your child is becoming frustrated with a certain concept, redirect his attention to something he is doing right and give him the desire to persevere.

Communicate clearly.

This sign was posted on a restroom door and illustrates

my point: TOILET OUT OF ORDER. PLEASE USE FLOOR BELOW. I have four boys who would take that sign for its literal meaning in a minute!

I cannot overemphasize how important clear communication is when teaching. Through lack of detail, we can distort the meaning of what we are saying. When working with your child, use step-by-step directions and plenty of details. Remember to have your child repeat the directions to you to ensure understanding.

Skip the "nots."

I have a challenge for you. Picture any animal in your mind right now, except a zebra. What was the first animal you saw?

Okay, another challenge. Do not yawn. Seriously, no yawning in the next minute. Keep fighting the urge to yawn. Do you get my point?

When you tell your child not to do something, you are stalling time because your child will automatically focus on the "not." Tell or show your child the correct method instead.

Here are some examples:

•Instead of saying, "Stop running around" try saying, "Please walk."

•Instead of saying, "You can't use a marker for that assignment" try saying, "I would like for you to use a

41

pencil for this assignment."

Use encouragement.

Anatolia France stated, "Nine tenths of education is encouragement."

That is a powerful quote. Encouraging your child means acknowledging progress, not just rewarding achievement. Continue to encourage your child frequently throughout a task to help him move toward finishing the assignment. Example: "I'm proud of you for completing X independently. Now, let's go on to Y."

Be specific when praising your child.

General praise is okay to use occasionally, but most praise should be specific when teaching. Always try to follow a simple phrase (general praise) with a detailed reason (specific praise). Example: "Fantastic! I like the way you _____."

Here is a list of over 80 ways to give general praise to your child. These are great lists to refer back to occasionally. Remember to follow them with specific praise.

You did it!
That's great!
Clear, concise, and complete!
Very creative!
That's a well-developed theme.
Very interesting!

Fantastic!
That's really nice.
Your style has spark.
Your work has such personality.
That's clever.
That's very perceptive.
You're right on target.
I like the way you've handled this.
I like the way you're working.
Good thinking!
Your work has pizzazz.
A splendid job!
You're right on the mark.
Good reasoning!
Very fine work!
You figured it out.
Outstanding!
I appreciate your help.
Keep up the good work.
I'm so proud of you.
You've made my day.
This is a winner!
Perfect!
You're on the ball today.
Superb!
This is something special.
What a hard-worker!
That's quite an improvement.
Superior work!
Great going!
Much better!
Wait until _____ sees this!
You're becoming an expert at this.
That's the right answer.

You're really moving on.
You're exactly right!
You're on the right track now.
What neat work!
Beautiful!
This is quite an accomplishment.
That's a good point.
You really outdid yourself today.
Super!
That's coming along nicely.
That's a very good observation.
Terrific!
This is prize-winning work.
Sensational!
I like your style.
Good for you!
You've really been paying attention.
You're really going to town.
That's an interesting point of view.
You've got it now.
You make it look so easy.
Nice going!
This shows you've been thinking.
Right on!
You've come a long way with this.
Top-notch work!
I appreciate your cooperation.
Marvelous!
This gets a five-star rating.
Excellent work!
Congratulations! You got ___ correct.
Magnificent!
WOW!
How impressive!

I commend you for your quick thinking.
Awesome!
The results were worth your hard work.
Nice Job!
I like the way you are working today.
Way to go!
I knew you could do it!

Have confidence in your child's ability.

Give your child the confidence he needs. For example, your child may be struggling and you may say, "I know this is hard, but I'm sure you can do it with just a little help. Let's start with one small part."

Emphasize effort.

Many parents fall into the trap of focusing on traits, such as "You're so smart." Instead, place your focus on your child's efforts, such as "I'm impressed with how hard you worked on that."

Remember to use enthusiasm when motivating your child to encourage more success. You are your child's primary role model. If you have an optimistic attitude towards learning, your child will likely have one, too.

Embrace mistakes.

Help your child understand that mistakes are an important part of learning. The process of trial and error is a natural component of success. After all, Thomas Edison maintained a positive outlook when it took him almost two years of failed attempts before he found success with his light bulb. Edison stated, "I have not failed. I've just found 10,000 ways that won't work. I am not discouraged because every wrong attempt discarded is often a step forward."

Your Challenge

I challenge you to choose one of these communication techniques that you would like to implement immediately. After you have developed a habit of using that technique consistently, practice using other techniques.

Chapter 3
Enlisting Support

You may feel like your child needs a tutor, in addition to the help you provide him at home. Many home educators often believe they have to teach every subject area themselves, but in reality, most parents are using tutors to teach subject areas they are not very enthusiastic about or do not feel knowledgeable enough in that subject area to teach their children.

Working with a tutor can free up extra time for you to work on other things while your child is being instructed. This approach can also motivate your child to work faster with an expert in a particular subject area since the tutor's instruction may be different. In addition, this approach may help your child get over an obstacle that is hindering his learning and slowing down his work pace.

For example, science experiments are difficult for me to do with my older children during this season of my life. My upper-elementary kids love to complete hands-on projects but so do my two toddlers who tend to mess up our projects once we get started. Therefore, I have learned how to be creative for the next couple of years until my younger children are old enough to participate in this part of homeschooling with us.

First, a close family friend who is majoring in science comes to our house once a week during the summer months to conduct hands-on science experiments. My kids are in awe when she teaches them. I usually take my two toddlers outside to play so my older kids can focus on the experiments without any interruptions from "Thing 1 and Thing 2."

Second, my husband does science experiments with my older kids during the school year at night, after the little ones go to bed. My husband has an engineering degree, so he enjoys exploring science projects with the boys. It is a great way for him to be involved with our homeschool lessons.

Third, my children attend a homeschool science class at the Edison Estates once a month that is led by the "Wild Wizard." This instructor is incredible and all the children in his classes are completely captivated. He makes learning stick like super glue, so it is completely worth my investment of money and time to drive them and wait during the classes. I usually take my little ones to a nearby playground, so they are very happy during science day.

I still teach my children science units during our school time, but as you can see, I enlist outside help to dive into the subject area more. I have learned my limitations and how to avoid future frustrations. By utilizing other options, my older kids still get plenty of opportunities to enjoy exploring science.

Another example of using a tutor is we have a piano instructor come to our house for piano lessons once a week. I do not know how to play the piano, so this is a big blessing for my children to learn from someone who has experience in that area.

Recognize the opportunities to use your strengths and when to ask for help during the times your child may need more instruction than you can offer him.

Tutoring for Academics

Sometimes tutoring is used to speed up the learning process by re-teaching skills the child has not mastered. This can get a child back to instructional level, so the parent can continue the learning process at home.

I had to use a tutor for my oldest son in mathematics. After trying repeatedly to help him over a wall in intermediate math and watching frustration set in for both of us, I sought help from another adult (who happened to be our neighbor). With some one-on-one instruction, my son was up and over that wall in a couple of months and I could resume teaching him math at home. Again, it is okay to ask for help when you need it.

What age should tutoring begin?

Children are born with an innate desire to learn, yet some children take longer to acquire school-readiness skills. Children are never too young to learn, but formalized tutoring should not take place before a child is six years old.

Because young children need stimulus and movement, it is not recommended that a child under age six be placed in formal, classroom-based instruction for tutoring purposes. An environment where children can learn naturally and retain their sense of wonder and curiosity, such as a playgroup, is preferred.

One to three hours per week in a hands-on playgroup would be appropriate for children under age six. In a playgroup, children find peers with similar abilities and feel more accepted. This type of early intervention can have a positive impact on the self-esteem of children.

How do you know if your child needs tutoring?

This is a question only you can answer. Whether your child is ready to surge ahead or simply needs to catch up, he can greatly benefit from tutoring. The answer will depend on if you can afford tutoring and is it a possibility with your family's schedule.

Offering a tutoring experience for your child is giving him an opportunity to excel in learning, but choosing a tutoring option that is a right match for your child can sometimes prove to be a little challenging. There are four important components that need to be considered when making a final decision to pursue tutoring for children six and older.

Talk to your child.

Have a discussion with your child about their learning. Ask your child questions, such as:

•Can you see the material?

•Can you hear me when I am teaching you?

•Are you frustrated? Why?

•Do you have a hard time sitting for long periods?

•Are there distractions at home that are causing you not to pay attention?

•Are you tired during school hours?

•Is the pace of learning too fast or too slow?

•Are you hungry during school hours?

•Do you ask me for help when you can't figure something out?

•What are your most and least favorite subjects? Why?

Please note that few tutors and tutoring centers are sufficiently equipped to handle students with learning disabilities. If you suspect your child has a learning disability or behavior problem, visit your child's pediatrician. He/she may offer advice and perform a diagnosis or send you to a specialist. If your child has been diagnosed with a learning disability, look for a private tutor who is a credentialed special-education teacher or has experience with teaching children with similarities as your child.

Realize learning is developmental.

If your child is taking longer than his peers to grasp concepts, do not panic. Take your time and progress at your child's own pace. The majority of learning that occurs in the elementary years is developmental, and there is not any conclusive evidence that early learners will perform better than their peers in future school years. No matter how much you push your child, he will not excel until he is developmentally ready.

The process of learning is like riding a bike. If your child is not developmentally ready to ride a bike, you are not going to put him on it day after day. You would take a break and pursue your child's other interests. You may wait a few weeks or months and try again. His friends may be riding their bikes for months or years before your child. However, your child may ride his bike faster and better than his friends when he finally masters that skill. Do not fall into the comparison trap. Strive to appreciate children's differences.

Do not use grades solely as your guide.

The primary indicator that your child is not making progress in school will be continued failing grades on your child's school work. I want you to realize that grades alone do not determine your child's ability and effort.

Earning a "C" means average progression! For some reason, parents' perceptions have evolved into believing a "C" in a subject means their child is struggling. They expect nothing lower than an "A." An "A" means exceptional and only a small percentage of students will honestly perform at this level.

As a former schoolteacher, I felt tremendous pressure from parents regarding grades. I repeatedly reminded parents that a "C" is good, and their child is on track and performing at an average rate since the current grading system is set for most learners to perform at a "C" level. Only when a child is performing below a "C" level for several months should intervention be considered.

When your child is trying his best in school, reward his effort, not his grades. Some of the hardest working and most well-behaved children I have taught were "C" students. As a teacher, it saddened me to see these children who tried their absolute best to open their report cards and look disappointed. This should not happen! They are intellectually performing at an average ability with exceptional behavior skills. These children should be commended for their hard work.

Straight-A children are typically high-achievers. High-achieving students are usually neat, well-rounded, hard workers. Adults comment on these students' consistent high grades and note how well they acclimate to classroom procedures.

Identification of gifted students is often clouded when adults misinterpret high achievement as giftedness. On the contrary, most of the "gifted" children I have taught were not straight-A children. These children were willing to take risks and think out-of-the-box. Unfortunately, they are penalized for this way of thinking in a standard grading system.

I believe all children are gifted because every child is a gift from God. Schools only test for giftedness in limited categories. It is your responsibility as your child's parent to help him discover his strengths and talents.

Many of the most brilliant minds in history were not A-students. Here are some examples:

"My teacher told me I'm not good at anything. She told me I'm mentally slow, unsociable, don't have any talent, and won't be successful in anything because I'm adrift forever in my foolish dreams."

~Albert Einstein, who is practically synonymous with "genius," widely regarded as the greatest scientist of the 20th century, and recipient of a Nobel Prize for physics.

"I was considerably discouraged by my school days. It was not pleasant to feel myself so completely outclassed and left behind at the beginning of the race." He was regularly punished in school for failure or lack of effort, sometimes failing the same class numerous times.

~ Winston Churchill, who is regarded as one of the greatest leaders in all of history, Prime Minister of the United Kingdom during World War II, journalist, author, politician, and recipient of the Nobel Prize for literature.

"I was always recognized as the slow one in the family. It was quite true, and I knew it and accepted it. Writing and spelling were always terribly difficult for me. My writing was without originality, and I was an extraordinarily bad speller and have remained so until this day."

~Agatha Christie, the great mystery writer who has sold over one billion books, which are more copies than anyone other than William Shakespeare.

"I was never able to get along at school. I was always at the foot of the class." His mother pulled him out of school and taught him at home. He gave his mother's homeschooling credit for his success in later life and said, "My mother was the making of me. She was so true, so sure of me; and I felt I had someone to live for, someone whom I must not disappoint."

~Thomas Edison, who is known as the most prolific inventor of all time, holding a record of 1093 patents.

I am not implying that grades do not matter at all. They are a good reference point for your child's progress, and you want to make sure your child is working up to his full potential. However, it is important for you to realize that grades should not be the sole indicator of your child's intellectual ability.

Help your child find his strengths and focus on those, not his grades. Remind him daily not to give up hope and that he is uniquely made by the Lord to accomplish great things in life. You are your child's biggest cheerleader!

You have options.

I was a tutor for twelve years and have seen all the advertising and media attention tutoring businesses receive. I'd like to inform you of all your tutoring options, including the simple and more cost efficient alternatives. With new technology and unique approaches being developed, there are a variety of tutoring options from which students and parents can choose. Knowing what your child specifically needs will help guide you towards the right tutoring option.

Many children require only a little extra attention and support. Some students need help with organization and study skills. Others need re-teaching to fill in the gaps of learning not yet mastered in previous years. Occasionally, a student requires intensive instruction and specialized strategies to overcome learning disabilities.

Regardless of which option you decide on for your child, make sure that positive reinforcement and encouragement are part of the teaching strategy. Simple words of encouragement can help build your child's self-esteem and confidence.

Option 1
Learn more effective teaching tools.

I encourage you to read my book *How to Teach Your Child*, which provides parents with practical, teaching methods in the core subject areas that actively engage children in the learning process. Learn how to enhance your current curriculum without experiencing burnout.

Option 2
Look into mentoring programs.

There are mentorship programs that involve pairing an older child or adult with a younger child to help facilitate the younger child's learning. Do you have any retired neighbors that would be interested in helping your child? Can your child's grandparents make weekly visits to instruct your child if they live locally? This quality time will be appreciated by both your child and his grandparents.

Pair up your child with an older child in the neighborhood or your child's homeschool group. You could also pay the older child a small amount of money as an incentive, which would be a minimal cost when compared to hiring a professional tutor. Not only could these people tutor your child, but they could mentor him as well by combining teaching with discipleship.

Option 3
Inquire about peer tutoring.

In this type of program, students work in groups and help each other with their assignments and studying for tests. Educators or older students from a higher grade level may volunteer to help facilitate the group. One perk is most peer tutoring programs are free.

Children enjoy the interaction with their peers and often learn better in a collaborative environment. In addition, working with other children with similar difficulties can help them realize that they are not the only ones struggling, which is often reassuring. Another benefit of participating in a peer tutoring group is the opportunity to develop positive social skills by working together towards a shared goal.

You could form your own group with children from your homeschool group or children in your neighborhood. I have a Bible Club with kids in my neighborhood who meet one night a week in my home. We learn Bible stories, recite scripture, and play games together. The kids love learning as a group, and they continually challenge one another.

Option 4
Swap with a friend.

Many parents are convinced their children listen more attentively to other adults better than themselves. If this is your scenario, consider swapping or sharing tutoring duties with a friend whose child has the same needs as your child. This is also excellent for teaching subject areas you feel inadequate in.

For example, I taught art classes to a small group of homeschooled children while another parent taught Spanish. I love art history and creating art projects and the other parent speaks Spanish fluently (I don't speak it at all), so this trade was a win-win for our children. The kids really enjoyed going to each other's homes and learning together.

Option 5
Hire a personal tutor.

One-on-one tutoring is among the most common types of instructional programs. If you have exhausted the above options, check with other home educators or your child's pediatrician for recommendations for a personal tutor. Tutors often place flyers at places like supermarkets, libraries, and recreation centers.

One unique way to find a tutor is to post a flyer at a nearby college. I often saw these posted on bulletin boards when I was attending college. Many students earning their education degrees are eager to apply for these positions to have more experience in their field, to practice new methods they are currently learning in their classes, and to earn some money in hours that work around their school schedule.

Contact volunteer organizations and ask family members and friends for recommendations of tutors they have used. Newspaper and phone directory advertisements can be helpful for finding a good tutor. Keep in mind that many phone directory ads may belong to larger tutoring or educational organizations rather than individual tutors.

Do not overlook the Internet as a place to look for a good tutor. Just type "tutor" in your favorite search engine, along with the name of your city, and sift through the results that appear. I even found my oldest son's guitar teacher by searching on Craigslist. Most importantly, look for a tutor willing to tailor his or her methods to meet the needs of your child.

Many parents opt for in-home tutoring instead of sending their students to a tutoring business. They feel more comfortable having their children tutored in familiar surroundings. Parents can protect their children and maximize the benefits from tutoring if they use this approach. Always meet the tutor before your first scheduled session and conduct reference checks.

If you are hiring a tutor through an agency, inquire that the agency has done the following:

•Interviewed the tutor face-to-face

•Conducted reference checks

•Performed the relevant child protection screening

•Researched the qualifications and experience of the tutor

You should be present during the tutoring session. This will eliminate the possibility of the tutor being left alone in your home with your child. Tutoring should never take place in the student's bedroom but in an open area where you can view and hear the process, such as the dining area or kitchen table.

As a professional tutor, I usually went to the children's location, whether it was their after-school program or their home. This helped the family avoid the wasted time spent driving and waiting. It also freed up extra hours that can be utilized for additional learning with the parents after I left.

A strategy that may be able to shorten your tutoring visits per week and save you money is to request the tutor gives your child extra work and provides you with direction in what to work on at home for the week. This will give you more confidence with helping your child since you will have a professional overseeing your child's progress.

If you are in contact with a certified teacher that would have time to tutor your child, barter with that person. For example, my hairdresser exchanges services with a tutor for her son. Other common practices I have personally seen are house cleaning, babysitting, automobile maintenance, and carpet cleaning services. These are great options for those parents who are on a tight budget.

Questions to ask

Education and experience

•Can you tell me what your qualifications and experience are, and how are they relevant to the area I am seeking tutoring in?

•Do you have a university qualification in the field of education?

•How long have you been tutoring/teaching this subject?

•Do you have clients I can call and ask about your tutoring services?

•Have you been screened for child protection purposes? May I see your paperwork?

Programs and reports

•Where do you tutor?

•How many times per week will you meet with my child?

•How long is a tutoring session? Are there breaks provided for sessions over 60 minutes?

•Do you follow a set program of study or curriculum?

•Will there be additional work expected of my child after each tutoring session?

•What learning styles are your teaching methods most compatible with?

•How often will I get verbal/written progress reports?

•If my child is not meeting your expectations, how will I know?

<u>Payment plan</u>

•What is the total cost of tutoring?

•What is the payment schedule?

•What is your preferred method of payment?

•If my child cannot or does not want to continue tutoring, will there be any cancellation fees or other charges applied?

Option 6
Research computer-based tutoring options.

There are several homeschool programs that provide computer-based instruction, such as Switched-On Schoolhouse, Teaching Textbooks, and even virtual schools. I have used these options when I did not have enough knowledge to teach my oldest son certain subject areas, such as higher math and grammar courses. I have also used many different video programs for math, science, and history.

Sometimes parents prefer tutoring assistance, in addition to the curriculum, through the use of computer programs. These computer-based options are quite appealing due to the lower costs when compared to hiring a personal tutor or enrolling their child in a tutoring center. Online tutoring services offer some of the benefits of private tutoring without the scheduling constraints. This tutoring option eliminates the burden of traveling, and it provides parents with peace of mind knowing strangers will not be coming into their homes.

Tutoring software can be completed anytime, anywhere. I have seen children completing their work on their laptops while a sibling was at soccer practice, as well as waiting for a doctor's appointment. If your child has an on-line program and a laptop with wireless Internet connection, he can complete it anywhere in your home and still be close to you in case he needs assistance.

Many educational companies make their programs seem more like a game, which helps motivate students and encourages them to continue their sessions. Most students are comfortable and familiar with computer-based technologies, and this type of tutoring gives children independence.

The methods used by on-line tutoring centers are similar to those used in traditional tutoring centers. A diagnostic test is given to determine what kind of help your child needs. A program is then customized for your child. In most cases, the programs are structured so that your child learns and reinforces skills from the bottom up. This ensures any gaps of learning your child may have are filled and mastered.

Keep in mind that computer-based technologies that are complemented by face-to-face tutoring have the best results for students. They can be guided into the appropriate use of the software and have effective and immediate remediation.

Questions to ask

•Does the age of my computer matter?

•Is the program compatible with my computer hardware and software?

•Does it make a difference if I have a Mac instead of a PC?

•Is my Internet connection fast enough?

•How often will I be required to download?

•Who wrote the software, and how does it relate to state standards?

•What does the course involve, and how it is expected to help my child?

•What is the cost of the program? Is this cost per session, week, month, or a one-time fee for the complete program?

•What method of payment is used? Be very careful about direct debit systems and understand the full implications of any contract before signing. If the company offers to finance the purchase, be aware of the full cost upfront and the large costs generally associated with such purchases.

•What technical and educational support is available for the course and how and when is it provided? Many educational software companies offer over the phone or on-line support for students. However, these rely on the student to initiate and are often run by untrained people. Be very clear about the service to which you are subscribing, and ask detailed questions about the nature of the support your child may receive if they require help.

Option 7
Check into local tutoring centers.

Tutoring centers are also called learning centers. I purposely listed this option last because of the costs and time involved. Most tutoring centers charge large fees that can quickly put a dent in a parent's budget. A family can pay up to $150 per week for services at a tutoring center depending on the number of hours a child needs assistance.

There are several benefits of using a tutoring center. There are diagnostic tests that are used to find out specifically your child's strengths and weaknesses, which allow the tutoring centers to develop an individualized learning strategy for your child. The program can be taught by any of the center's employees, so your child won't miss a session because his tutor is sick. Students can benefit from group tutoring by helping and learning from each other, and small groups can allow for individual study time.

Time is a major consideration with an average of three visits per week. You have to factor in the time for transportation to and from the location and the time waiting. When you have more than one child, this is an issue since you have to plan activities to occupy your other children.

Some other aspects of tutoring centers to consider are families cannot choose a specific tutor to work with, and your child is less likely to build a rapport and close relationship with his tutor because of the revolving tutors. The tutors generally work with three to five students at the same time, so the tutor's attention will be divided and individual attention will be limited. In addition, your child may be embarrassed if he is struggling with problems in front of others.

Please consider your child's best learning times when scheduling the appointment time. Remember your child may be restless from sitting all day. Offer your child breaks in between and encourage physical activity beforehand.

Questions to ask

<u>Education and experience</u>

•How long have you been in business?

•May I have the names of other parents that I can talk to about the quality of your tutoring services?

•What are the qualifications and experience requirements of those who will be tutoring my child?

•Are the tutors trained specifically in the subject area in which they are tutoring?

•Have reference checks been conducted on the tutors?

•Have relevant child protection screenings been performed on the tutors?

Programs and reports

•Do you follow formal school curriculum or have your own program?

•Can I view your curriculum/program?

•How will your program be relevant to my child?

•Is there any additional work expected of my child in the form of homework or after hours study?

•How often do you give reports on my child's progress?

•What other intervention methods do you use if my child does not seem to be benefiting from your program?

Operations

•Where will the tutoring take place?

•May I view the tutoring when it takes place? If not, is there a waiting area for parents?

•Is the tutoring one-to-one or in a group? If it is a group situation, how large is it and how will the needs of my child be individually addressed?

Contract conditions and fees

•What is your preferred method of payment? Be very careful about direct debit systems and understand the full implications of any contract before signing. If the company offers to finance the purchase, be aware of the full cost upfront and the large costs generally associated with such purchases.

•How much can I expect to pay in total for the tuition?

•Do you provide discounts, financial aid, or scholarships? Most centers do not advertise these price reductions even though they are available.

•What will happen if my child is unhappy or we want to cancel the tutoring? Are there any cancellation fees or additional charges?

•Do you have a refund policy?

•How much notice will I have to give in order to not be charged for a session of tutoring due to illnesses or family emergencies?

•Will I be required to pay for any additional support materials or books?

When you sign a contract for tutoring services, you are legally bound by its terms and conditions and usually cannot back out. Always read carefully any document you are asked to sign. If you don't understand it, don't sign it.

Learning is a process.

These tutoring options are not a quick-fix. Please keep in mind that progress may take some time to occur. If you do not see any progress with your child's academic performance in six months, reevaluate other possible hindrances, such as: learning styles, methods of motivation, nutritional deficiencies, and sleep patterns.

The most effective tutoring helps students literally learn "how to learn." Your ultimate educational goal for your child should be for him to become an independent learner and work up to his full potential. A love of learning begins at home with parents who care about their child's academic progress and do their best to create a positive learning environment. Remember, you are your child's most influential teacher. Keep inspiring and motivating your child to reach for new heights.

Chapter 4
Learning on the Go

As a "home" school mom, there are some days I am rarely home. There may be doctor, dentist, and orthodontist appointments. Some days we have music lessons, sports practices, and church functions. Let's not forget about the homeschool co-op events and the opportunities to serve others. Not to mention, "life" that pops up and derails our pristine lesson plans that once looked perfect in our planning books.

So what happens on these days? We just learn on the go. Here are 50 simple tricks I have learned to add pizzazz to our time in the car and while waiting for appointments. My kids bring their school work with us and we turn the world into our classroom.

Links to stores that sell most of the products mentioned in this chapter can be found on my site if you'd like to learn more about them. Just click on the store link at the very bottom of the "resources" tab.

Language Arts

Mystery writing- If you have more than one passenger in the car, have them write words with their fingers on each other's backs and try to guess them. Children can also close their eyes, and write on each other's forearms.

Spelling bee- Call out words to your child. You can use spelling words or words on signs and billboards while you are traveling.

Magnetic madness- Use a cookie sheet or a magnetic board and a collection of alphabet magnets to make words.

Drawing boards- Using an Etch-A-Sketch or a Magna Doodle are fun ways to draw in the car. Your child can even practice writing his spelling words.

Amazing alphabet- Try to locate each letter of the alphabet in order from signs, billboards, license plates, and so on. For a variation, find as many things as you can that begin with a certain letter. Attempt to go through the entire alphabet for a challenge.

First and last- Choose a category, such as places, names, foods, or animals. Have your child begin with a word that fits the category. The next player has to say a word that begins with the last letter of the previous word. For example, the category is animal. The words can be mouse, elephant, tiger, rhinoceros, sheep, and so on.

Mad Labs- Use these word game booklets to practice the parts of speech with a twist of silliness.

What am I? - Call out a word. Have your child name the parts of speech, such as: noun, pronoun, adjective, verb, adverb, preposition, conjunction, and interjection.

Rhyme time- Call out a word, and see how many words your child can think of that rhyme with it.

Syllable search- Call out a word. Have your child say the number of syllables the word has. Have your child clap or snap the rhythm if needed. You can make this more challenging by searching for objects that have a particular number of syllables. For instance, the chosen number is two. You can get points if you drive by a Camry, billboard, and stoplight.

Word train- The first person says a word for the beginning of a sentence. The next person says the first word and then adds another word. You keep adding words to form a silly sentence. A person can also say a punctuation mark, such as a period, when it is time to end the sentence. The next person starts a new sentence.

Storytelling- All the people in the car take turns telling part of a story, adding on to it as you go.

Story time- Have your child read books aloud. Riddle books and question and answer books are particularly fun because everyone can participate in guessing the correct answers.

Daily devotions- Have your child read aloud from a children's devotional.

Comedy corner- Fill your car with laughter by having your child read aloud from a joke book.

Audio books- Public libraries have audio books for all ages. While your child is listening to the story, stop the cassette or CD. Ask your child to predict what will happen next. You can also discuss the story elements: setting, main characters, plot, and conclusion.

Mathematics

Where in the world are we? - Have your child trace with a crayon or colored pencil on a map the path you are driving. Teach him how to use the map's scale to estimate the number of miles you need to travel to your destination.

Meandering miles- Predict the number of miles it will be from one place to another. Click on your odometer to see who wins.

Are we there yet? - Guess what exact time you will arrive at your destination. Check your clock to see who is the closest.

Math Shark- Using a Math Shark is the best way I have found to drill math facts. Give a specific goal, and set a time limit for your child, such as complete the addition facts for nines in less than sixty seconds.

Counting games- Count police cars, motorcycles, types of automobiles, cows, stoplights, churches, billboards, people, specific letters and numbers, and so on.

Patterning- Begin a number pattern. Have your child complete it, such as 3, 6, 9, ___.

Geoboards- Have your child creates different geometric shapes and objects with rubber bands using Geoboards.

Battleship- Two passengers individually draw two grids with 10x10 squares on graph paper. Label one grid "My ship" and the other "Opponent's ship." Write the letters (A-J) on the vertical axis and the numbers (1-10) on the horizontal axis. Each player shades in five squares in a row to represent his ship on the "My ship" grid.

The players take turns calling out a spot on the grid using the letter and the number, such as A5. The other player says "hit" if his ship is on that spot or "miss" if it is not. Players keep track of the guesses by writing an H for a hit or an M for a miss on the grid labeled "Opponent's ship." If a player guesses correctly all the squares for a ship, that ship is considered sunk, and the opposing player says, "You sunk my battleship." What an entertaining way to practice coordinate points in graphing!

Math songs- Have your child listen to and sing math songs on cassette or CD, such as skip counting, addition, and multiplication songs.

Geography

License plate game- The goal of this challenging game is to find all of the United States' license plates (excluding Hawaii & Alaska). Print from the Internet or make your own outline map of the United States with just the names of the states labeled. Place the U.S. map on a clipboard, and leave it in the car. Use a highlighter to shade in a state when your child sees the corresponding license plate. Work as a team to see how many states' license plates you can find.

Map it- Give your child paper and a pencil. Have him make his own map of where you are going. Draw the major landmarks, bridges, churches, stoplights, train tracks, and so on.

Geography songs- Have your child listen to and sing geography songs on cassette or CD.

Creative Arts

Aluminum foil art- Leave a roll of aluminum foil in your car. Have your child mold it into anything he wants, such as animal shapes, balls, jewelry, and masks.

Pipe cleaner art- Give your child a bag of multi-colored pipe cleaners, and let his creativity run wild. He can make flowers, animals, chains, letters, and jewelry.

String figures- Give your child a piece of string or yarn. See if he can make "Jacob's Ladder," "Kitty Whiskers," or "Cup and Saucer." If your child needs a crash course on string figures, check out *Cat's Cradle* by Anne Akers Johnson.

Critical Thinking Skills

Brain Quest- These question and answer cards are a fabulous learning tool that can be used in the car or while waiting at places, such as doctor's offices and restaurants. The questions are on one side of the card, and the answers are on the next card, so children can play Brain Quest alone or with others.

Scavenger hunt- Give your child a list of certain objects to look for, such as: barn, bike, bird, bus, cell phone, church, cow, dirt road, dog, flashing red light, gas station, person walking, playground, pond, school, statue, stop sign, store, and tractor.

Who am I? - Think of someone you know, friend or relative. Describe that person by using details, such as she has blond hair, blue eyes, and likes to sing. Keep giving clues until someone guesses the correct person.

Portable educational games- These interactive games, such as Leapfrog's Leap Pad Learning System and Leapster, are excellent alternatives to the popular Nintendo DS.

Fascinating favorites- Take turns naming your favorites, such as: color, food, movie, song, and restaurant. To make this more challenging, try to guess each other's favorites.

Play classical music- This is an excellent way for you and your child to unwind and relax after a stressful day. Classical music can reduce heart rate, blood pressure, breathing rate, stress, and anxiety. *The Mozart Effect* by Don Campbell is a comprehensive review of hundreds of studies between 1972 and 1992 that found classical music aids in reading, language, mathematics, and overall academic achievements.

Just for Fun

Traveling bingo- You can make your own bingo cards or purchase ready-made traveling bingo cards. These can be quite entertaining if you have more than one child in the car.

Educational DVDs- If you have a DVD player available in your car, check out educational DVDs from your public library and play them.

Lacing shapes- Your child can sew lacing shapes while improving fine-motor skills.

Going on a picnic- The first person says, "I am going on a picnic, and I am taking a _____," and names something that begins with the letter "A." The next person repeats the phrase with the first item and adds something that begins with letter "B."

The pattern continues until someone becomes stumped on thinking of an item that begins with a certain letter or someone forgets the items in the correct order. (It becomes a challenge trying to recall all the items.) Younger children can name items that start with the same letter, such as all the items begin with the letter "A." They do not need to remember the items that were before their turn.

You can also revise the game by changing the settings, such as "Going Camping." You play the game in the same fashion but instead you say, "I am going camping, and I am taking a _____."

Crazy clouds- What do the clouds look like? Use your imaginations to find different shapes and objects in the sky.

Silly sounds- Make sounds for different things when you drive by them, such as ding-dong, moo, beep-beep, and so on. Be prepared to laugh at the sound effects.

Rainbow game- Call out a color. See how many things you can find of that color.

Classics

Tic-Tac-Toe- If you have more than one passenger in the car, let them have fun with the Xs and Os.

I Spy- Look around and pick an object you can see in the car or along the road. Give a clue, such as, "I spy with my little eye...something furry and brown." Continue to give more clues until someone guesses the correct answer. The person who guesses correctly gets to think of the next object.

Name that tune- Switch radio stations quickly to play parts of songs, and try to guess the name of them. You can also take turns humming the tune of different songs and guessing them.

Rock, Paper, Scissors- As you count to three, lightly pound your fist into the palm of your hand. Turn your fist into an object of your choice on "three." There are three objects to choose from: rock (a closed fist), paper (an open palm), or scissors (two fingers in a sideways V shape). A rock wins by crushing scissors, paper wins by covering the rock, and scissors win by cutting paper. If two people have the same objects, they can go again.

Twenty questions- Think of an object that is a common noun. "Is it a person, place, or thing?" is the first question asked. The players can ask anything they want as long as you are able to answer yes or no to their questions. Encourage your child to ask questions that will narrow down the choices. If someone guesses the correct object in less than twenty questions, he wins.

Coloring- With our fast-paced culture and all the technology that surrounds us, coloring for fun has become a forgotten pastime. Coloring is excellent for fine motor skills. Let's revive this activity by keeping a coloring book and crayons accessible to our children. (You may have to substitute coloring pencils for crayons if you live in a warm climate.) You can also have mazes and dot-to-dots available.

Learning does not always have to take place in your home at a table but view the world as your classroom. Have fun with these travel games. Your child may be begging you to hit the road more often!

Chapter 5
Making Time for You

Have you ever felt like you experienced an identity crisis? Perhaps you realized it like I did when I was in a room with fellow home educators and the introductions began. This is what happened to me two years ago. When it was my turn to introduce myself, I said my typical response. "Hello. I'm Tamara Chilver. I have five children ranging in ages from 4 months to 17. I have been homeschooling for 13 years."

Now this is where I tried my best to say something interesting about myself. I paused and pondered. I began to question who I had become. Did I have any interests and dreams left? There had to be at least one interesting thing about myself. Nope, nada. My mind went blank. Sleep deprivation must have been taking its toll. Who was I? That is when I knew...

There has been an identity theft!

Have you been here before? If you cannot think of any interests to share or cannot describe who you are besides using the nouns "mom, wife, caretaker, home educator, and Christian," it could be time to reclaim your identity as well.

My identity crisis began after my fifth child. Homeschooling three older children and caring for two babies in diapers took every bit of my time, but I recognized it was only for a season. After I could catch my breath, I began to get to know myself again. It was a process but I finally reclaimed my identity.

Get to know yourself again.

Mothers spend lots of time helping their children achieve their dreams and desires, such as in sports, hobbies, playing instruments, art classes, and so on. This is why it is imperative that mothers set the example for their children and carve out a little time to pursue their passions, too.

One of my favorite scriptures is Psalm 37:4, "Delight yourself in the Lord, and He shall give you the desires of your heart."

This is the scripture I prayed over when I was recovering from my identity theft. I asked God to fill my heart with His desires. I wanted to have dreams and passions again. Here I was at home not able to go many places since I had nap and feeding cycles alternating between an infant and a one-year-old all day long. I was also homeschooling my three older children.

Our closest relatives lived hours away so we learned to rely more on each other to make things work. My oldest son took my two middle sons to homeschool classes and events, as well as appointments. My husband and I would alternate watching the kids and running errands and grocery shopping. Any speaking opportunities to homeschool groups and television contributions came to a halt, yet I still had a burning desire to encourage others. How could God possibly use me to help others when I could hardly get out of my pajamas and take a shower?

After praying over Psalm 37:4 for a few weeks, God showed me how to encourage parents from home through the Internet. I began an educational collaborative site that literally exploded overnight and had millions of page impressions. It quickly became the highest ranked educational blog on the web at that time. I received emails and prayer requests from people around the world. It was absolutely amazing!

I was in awe that God could use me to encourage so many people from my home while in my pajamas with a baby sitting on my lap as I typed. What a powerful testimony that demonstrates God can use anyone despite our current circumstances. All we have to do is seek Him and ask for His plan, wisdom, and grace.

I encourage you to get to know yourself again and start believing that God places dreams and desires in your heart for you to follow and enjoy. Please do not feel guilty that you are spending some time on yourself. You are God's child and He wants you to enjoy your life just as you want your child to enjoy his.

So who am I now?

I have regained my identity and now can tell you more about myself than I could two years ago. When I look into the mirror, I see a smiling mom often wearing a ponytail and flip-flops. I am an organizational freak and a girl who is in love with Jesus. The things that make me the happiest are eating at Cracker Barrel, a large

McDonald's tea, chocolate chip cookies made from scratch, vacations with my family, date nights with my hubby, and hanging out with my girlfriends.

I am a huge sweet tooth and enjoy baking with my kids. I like scrap-booking even though I feel like I will be forever behind. Since I was a little girl, I have dreamed of living in a log cabin nestled in the Smoky Mountains.

I love walking in the mornings and use it as my prayer time and a time to get revitalized for the school day. I like being surrounded by nature and often get some of my best ideas for writing and homeschooling during those walks. If I did not allow myself time to exercise and prepare for the day, I would suffer but so would my children. They need a healthy mother. We must take care of our bodies physically and spiritually to be the best provider for our precious children.

I am passionate about serving others. I enjoy helping and encouraging friends, family, and homeschool moms, and I am thankful when God is using my strengths to bless others. If I filled up my days with homeschooling, I would be closing the door to opportunities that God could use me. This is why we must manage our homeschool time wisely and set aside time to open our hearts and homes to others. It is what being a follower of Christ is really all about.

Now it's your turn. Who are you?

What are your desires? Do you enjoy gardening, sewing, baking, scrap-booking, or painting? When you were younger, what did you envision yourself doing at your age now?

Here are some challenges for you:

•Rediscover an older passion and put a plan into action for it.

•Experiment and try something new. Create a bucket list and get adventurous.

•Spend time with girlfriends, without children around, at least once a month. This can be at a homeschool meeting, a Ladies' Bible Study, or a dinner with a friend celebrating a special occasion.

•Take a short walk. Sunshine and fresh air will do wonders for you.

•Have date nights with your spouse. Be creative and ignite your passion for each other.

Enjoy the journey.

Try not to rush through the school day or even your homeschool journey. Learning is not about the end product, such as graduation from high school or college, but it is a life-long process. I was surprised to learn that 42% of people that graduate from high school or college will never read a complete book the rest of their lives. It's because they view learning as a period in life instead of a way of life. Get your child hooked on learning for life. "The wise person makes learning a joy." Proverbs 15:2

Remember to seek God daily and ask for His guidance and wisdom in managing your time. The days often go by slow, but the years go by fast.

Thank you for giving me the opportunity to share my love of learning with you. I hope you have enjoyed these time-saving tips and will soon have much more time to devote to your passions and to enjoy your homeschool journey.

You are invited to visit me anytime for encouragement and fun teaching tips at *www.teachingwithtlc.com*. I have lots of resources, videos, and creative teaching tips that you may enjoy.

Please take a minute to write a sentence or two wherever you purchased this book to let me know how you liked it. Whenever I hear back from my readers through a review, it is like opening a present. I get so excited!

A Surprise for You!

I have an exclusive surprise just for the readers of this book! One of my favorite workshops that I have presented to several homeschool groups across the country is called *Buckets of Fun: Creative Teaching Tips to Splash Excitement into Your School Day*. Visit tinyurl.com/bucketsworkshop to begin your free audio recording of the workshop. Enjoy!

About the Author

Tamara L. Chilver is a popular homeschool author and an influential blogger who is passionate about providing parents with fun and creative teaching tips. Tamara's bachelor's degree is in elementary education, and her master's degree is in elementary curriculum. Before entering the homeschooling world 16 years ago with her five children, Tamara was a public school elementary teacher, a private school curriculum coordinator, and a private tutor. Tamara uses her diverse background in education to empower parents with confidence while simplifying learning methods. She is currently a speaker, television contributor and a best-selling author.

Additional Resources

How to Teach Your Child addresses one of the most common concerns homeschool moms have - How do I teach my child? Tamara L. Chilver reveals the tools of the trade while providing parents with simple teaching tips in the core subject areas that actively engage children in the learning process.

In this practical guide, you will learn how to:

•Make learning FUN.
•Enhance your existing curriculum.
•Use successful teaching tips.
•Prevent burnout for you and your child.
•Save money by using practical teaching tips.

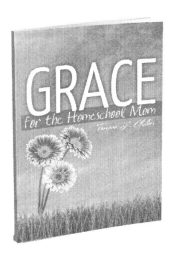

Goodbye worry, fear, doubt, and guilt. Hello grace.

Grace for the Homeschool Mom serves as the apologetics for the homeschool mom. This concise guide addresses the most common lies, fears, temptations, traps, and pitfalls that homeschool moms face. Use this book as a reference to arm yourself with God's grace and His Word to rcbuke the deceptions of the enemy. Break away from the enemy's bondage and begin to experience peace and freedom in your homeschool journey right away.

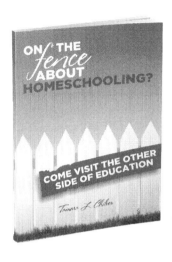

Do you find yourself sitting on the fence between traditional education options and homeschooling? Are you sensing God might be calling you to homeschool? Is fear keeping you from exploring your options?

Let Tamara Chilver gently guide you through the homeschool world in *On the Fence About Homeschooling?* As a former school teacher and now a veteran homeschool educator, she shares her personal journey with you while giving you the benefits, along with the sacrifices of homeschooling. After reading this book, you will be able to more confidently make a decision concerning the path that is best for your family.

Transform your child's spelling and writing lessons with these creative tips in *101 Ways to Make Spelling Fun* and *101 Ways to Make Writing Fun*. Why make learning fun? Research consistently shows that children learn more when they are actively engaged in the learning process and having fun.

Created for preschoolers up to sixth graders these engaging activities can be used as a stand-alone or as a compliment to any curriculum. There are activities that address all types of learning styles. These modern and lively writing and spelling assignments cross into many subject areas, including: reading, writing, math, music, government, and art. But let's not forget that these activities are just plain fun!

Simplify Your Homeschool Day

We offer quality shirts in a variety of color options and sayings.

www.homeschooltshirt.com